Lost in the Post

Dispatches From Inside
Her Majesty's Postal Service

Kevin Boniface

with photographs by Shaw and Shaw

First published in Great Britain 2008 by Old Street Publishing Ltd,
28–32 Bowling Green Lane, London EC1R 0BJ, UK
www.oldstreetpublishing.co.uk

Copyright in the text © Kevin Boniface 2008
web.mac.com/victorygarden.mac
Copyright in the images © Shaw and Shaw Images Ltd. 2008
www.shawandshaw.co.uk

Kevin Boniface is hereby credited as the finder of the
'Found Notes' featured in the pages of this publication.

A CIP catalogue record for this book is available
from the British Library.

ISBN13: 978 1905847 53 2

Printed and bound in Italy

10 9 8 7 6 5 4 3 2 1

DEDICATION

"...that's what you need." — Roy Castle.

LETS ALL GET TOGETHER
IN COMMUNION SWEET
WALK WALK IN THE LIGHT
LETS LOVE ONE ANOTHER TILL
THE SAVIOUR WE MEET
WALK WALK IN THE LIGHT
WALK IN THE LIGHT (REPEAT TWICE)
WALKING IN THE LIGHT OF GOD

My boss ran me out to the start of my delivery. As we drove by a school he nodded towards a man walking up the pavement. "You can tell he's a teacher," he said, "he's wearing gloves…"

In Holme Close a man was sweeping his lawn with a dustpan and brush.

As I crossed the health centre car park in Shellwood a man hurried across to intercept me. He grabbed my arm, pointed out one of the parked cars, and said, "That's one of them new number plates that is."

When I finally got to Radcliffe Post Office the queue was being held up by a frustrated customer who couldn't make himself understood. It turned out he was from the Congo and spoke French, so the woman behind the counter said, "Je m'appelle Christine" — and he left.

I Like

you christing

Missing Hamster

Name: Scratchy
Animal: Albino Syrian Hamster
Looks: Pure white with red eyes.
Help: If you find Scratchy, give him a carrot for he may be hungry.

If you find Scratchy please call: **0161 4480911**

Al's leaving do was in full swing when I arrived on my break. In the smoking room, Rod Singleton said he was surprised nobody had touched the carrots as they were gorgeous.

At the Grimscar box two teenage girls asked me if they could touch my van for good luck. I said they could. They touched the post box too.

```
✓   TAKODA      2 30   YORK
✓   THAKAFAAT   3 05   Y
✓   DARSALAM    3 45   Y
✓   TSA ROXY    4 20   Y
✗   HALLHOO     4 55   Y
2   LOOK HERE'S CAROL  5 30   Y

1   LIGHT METER  2 45   NEW
2   WAVETREE WORRIER  3 20   Y
1      SIR BLUEBIRD  3 55   Y
✓      TAWQEET         4 30   Y
2   ROCK CHICK       5 05   Y
1   INDIAN BAZAAR    5 40   Y
```

I saw a massive man watching telly in his front room as I queued in traffic outside his house.

The girl at the newsagent told me they'd got a new supplier of flapjack. She said not to worry though as the new stuff looked dead nice.

CHIPS

80 P

CRISPS

OIL

Someone had shoved a copy of today's *Sun* newspaper and the current issue of *Uncut* magazine into the post box on Grimscar.

At the Blackstone Mill box an old man who smelt strongly of Vicks Synex was posting a letter.

The receptionist at Copeland Marketing said, "Hello Mr Posty, have you brought me any sweeties?"

I said I hadn't.

In the smoking room Rod Singleton said the Fire Brigade don't allow car manufacturers to fit toughened glass because it's hard to break in an emergency. He thought this unfair and said he'd be prepared to take the risk if it would bring down his insurance premium. He said, "Firemen are fucking cunts."

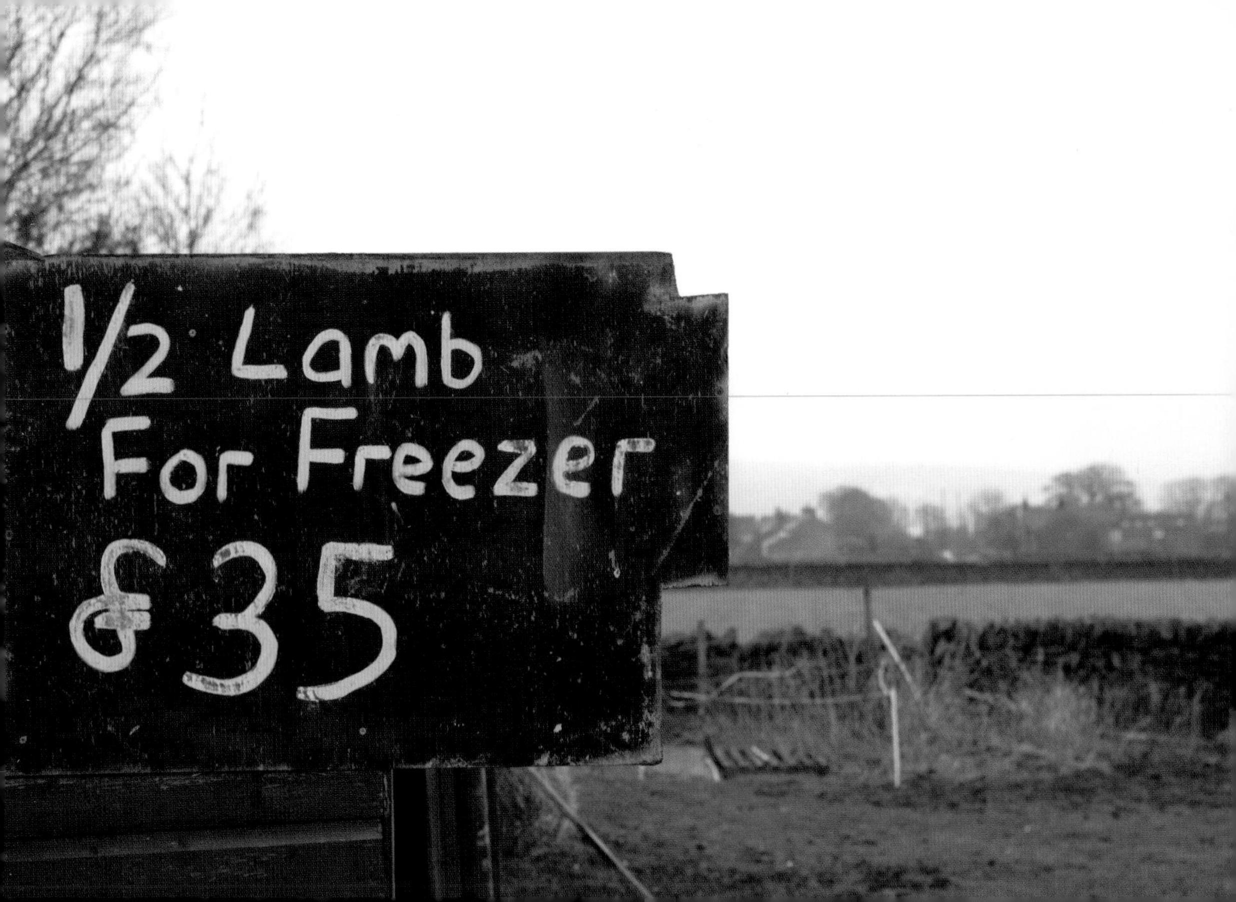
1/2 Lamb
For Freezer
£35

When I arrived at work I noticed a very cleanly severed pigeon's head on the pavement outside the gates to the yard. I couldn't see its body anywhere.

Mad Dog said he'd dreamt he'd been to see Van Halen live but Eddie Van Halen wasn't called Eddie Van Halen he was called John. He said they still rocked though.

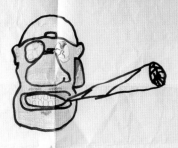

The wobbly, rapidly ageing, 1980s New Romantic man who hangs about outside the phone box on Dunford Bank was looking particularly wobbly today. He was trying to show off in front of his incongruous, bum-fluffed and Burberried-up companion by walking along some concrete bollards — but he kept falling off. His waistcoat was cool though.

In the *Evening Post* I noticed a story about a local baptist who ran a joinery where the face of Christ had manifested itself in a knot in a wooden door.

He said he'd sell it for sixteen pounds.

It'd been a fine, humid day and I was in my shirt sleeves when I was stopped in the street by a young black man with unusual wet-look hair and a Fair-Isle sweater squashed under a denim jacket done up as far as the top two studs. He ministered to me in the name of Islam for about three or four minutes. He didn't make eye contact once. He asked me to consider that if I hadn't accepted Allah as the one true God by the time of my death I'd be cast into Hell for all eternity. I said I'd bear it in mind and thanked him for his consideration.

When I got back to the yard an enthusiastic group discussion was taking place on the landing. Everyone was in broad agreement that celebrity chef Gordon Ramsay was "hard as nails". The conversation was interrupted when an elderly Asian man ran passed the gates pursued by a young white woman. The woman cornered him and harangued him for a couple of minutes. She screamed incoherently — stuff about the IRA, political stuff etc etc. In the end she accused the man of "lovin' it", tore off her top, and urged him to rape her — which he didn't.

Justin. michael·C.

Holly
L♡Z
Rik.

Danielle
L♡Z ← Slag
Cheesey.

Gina
L♡Z
Luke.

Sophie
L♡Z
Aaron.

Linzi
L♡Z
Swampy.

Kelsie
L♡Z
Buckley.

Harriet
L♡Z
Kenyon.

Jade
L♡Z
Jay.

Food
Milk
Cigs
Toilet rolls

On Old Yew Avenue a woman was leaning out of a window shouting down to a neighbour in the street: "... she said she was off up to the shop to get some toilet-roll. Her sister's coming over so she was going to have to get some toilet-roll in — in case she needs a wee."

I saw an old man covered in grass stains walking his terrier.

As I was pulling out of the gates to the yard I saw a man surreptitiously slipping a dead pigeon into his jacket pocket. I wondered whether this was a clue to the mystery of the severed pigeon head?

Later, on the landing, I told Ady about the Dead Pigeon Man. He told me about his mate's granddad who was so poor he used to go out on a Friday night and collect bits of meat from pools of sick in the street and fry them up when he got home.

A man who was encouraging his Staffordshire Bull Terrier to attack the branch of a tree asked me for a light as I emptied the Grimscar box. Inside the box I found copies of *TV Mag* and the *Sun*.

At the Dunford Bank box on my teatime collection the proprietor of the haberdashery was smoking a cigarette while he locked up his shutters. It had been raining all day.

"Fucking lovely weather isn't it?" he said as he yanked at the cord that secured his awnings. "If you're a fucking duck," he added.

He stood up and nodded towards the sofa shop proprietor next door who was carrying in some potted ferns for the night.

"Oh well, I'd better go give him a hand loading this fucking chair into his van. See yer."

In the smoking room Rod Singleton said people who rob Post Offices should be tied to lamp posts and flogged with broom handles by half a dozen or so postmen. "Don't hit their faces though — then people won't be able to see the damage," he explained. "If the police arrive, all the postmen should blame each other and then say, 'Pick the bones out of that — you cunts.'"

Rod said that people are too soft nowadays and that there are too many do-gooders about.

At Town End office the postmistress asked me, "Have you always had a beard or is it just me?"

As I was waiting to scan the Grimscar box the tall thin man who was walking up the road towards me dropped his keys and Cadbury's Twirl on the floor. He was on his phone so he tried to pick them up one-handed. He picked up the Twirl first then attempted to retrieve his keys with just his index and middle fingers. He fumbled for a couple of seconds and eventually managed it – only to drop them again as he straightened up. He bent down again and repeated the procedure with the same results. He bent down a third time and tried a variety of approaches including: lodging the phone under his chin (he gave up on this when he nearly dropped that as well); lodging the Twirl under his arm and crouching (he still couldn't reach); and finally putting the Twirl back down on the ground and starting again with the keys. This eventually worked.

13,201   Clothes

1 trousers . ✓

2 Skirt ✓ $8\frac{1}{2}$

3 Shoes . ✓   ─────

4 Coat ✓ $\overline{10}$

5 Dress . ✓

6 tie ✓   ~~1pt~~

7 Socks . ✓

8 un Pull . ✓

9 un ~~Jean~~ Jeans . $\frac{1}{2}$

10 - " une   C   ✗

On the landing Paul advised other Paul to put up his dado rail using No More Nails. He said he wouldn't trust it with anything else though. Paul said he knew a place you can get massive tubs of No More Nails "cheap as chips".

The proprietor of the haberdashery came out as I was about to clear the pillar box just outside his shop.

"I'm fed-up with fucking customers who rock-up as I'm about to lock up at five-to-fucking-five," he said. "Last night it was twenty-to-cunting-six before I finally got away. I'd run out of cigs and the newsagent was shut. I wouldn't normally mind but I'd had a bastard day and then no cunt would let me get away."

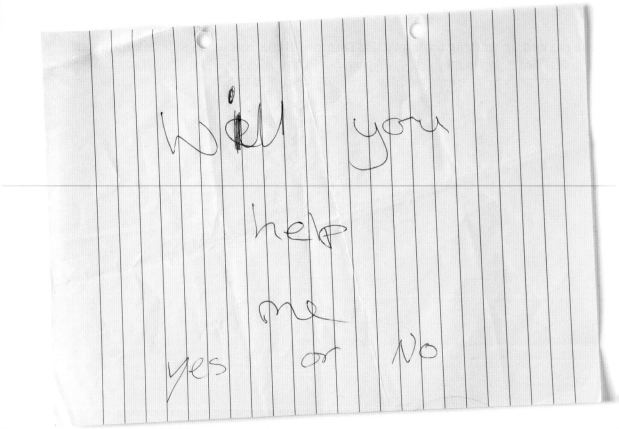

I was parked up waiting to empty the Dunford Bank box when a drunk man with bad teeth and very white trainers tapped on my window. I wound it down, and he offered me a pound to give him a lift to the top of the hill. I declined, and he staggered slowly off up the road.

When I ride home at night I always see the same man walking down Staniforth Road. He's Asian, about thirty-five to forty years old, moustache, beanie hat, shell suit top and jeans. After a few weeks we started to acknowledge each other with a cursory nod as we passed.

After a while longer this developed into a polite "Evening" and a small, salute-style wave.

It has now evolved into a full sweep-above-the-head wave accompanied by a loud "how do'?" I nearly fell off my bike doing it tonight.

MORNING
fellas

CAN YOU SEE IT?
ITS ON 1 —
SAME AS YESTERDAY!!!
THANKS — JOHN
xxx

I arrived at work at 5.15am and found a group of about 20 colleagues huddled together in the yard watching a couple having sex in the church yard opposite. The couple, oblivious to their audience, performed a drunken act of fellatio followed by full sexual intercourse. When they'd finished and were pulling up their underwear they were applauded and cheered loudly.

He seemed more embarrassed than her and ran off quickly to join some mates who'd been waiting for him at the bus stop round the corner. She just flicked a "V" sign and walked off in the opposite direction.

I was driving down Southern Road when I stopped for an old lady with a dog who'd decided to cross really slowly without looking. When they got to the middle, the dog stopped to have a shit and the old lady wasn't strong enough to pull it out of the way. Queues of about a dozen cars had built up in both directions before they got to the other side.

There was a small portion of furry chips inside the Grimscar box.

Rod Singleton said he'd been to Comet to buy a new telly. "I always go to Comet for my telly stuff," he said. "They tried to sell me one of those plasma TV jobs. It was amazing, it had everything for the serious cinema goer — even a chair with some little buttons in the arm so you could just sit there and go peew peew." Rod mimed going "peew peew" on the torn vinyl upholstery of his 1970s-smoking-room chair, and went on, "I asked the fella how much it was and he said two-and-a-half-thousand pounds. I said, 'What! I'm only a postman you soft cunt!'"

The proprietor of the Bizmillah blocked me in again. This time outside Dunford Bank office. He pulled his Nissan Micra right up to my bumper and then pretended to shoot me through the windscreen with his index and middle fingers. He seemed to think this was the funniest thing ever.

As I rode home from work I passed three well-tanned drunks accompanied by two bull terriers. They were inspecting a bin-liner full of board games. "What the fuck's this?" said one, holding up a game to the light of a street lamp. "Hey that's Mouse Trap that is, we used to play that when I was a kid," said another.

As I rounded the corner into Station Street I was surprised by the number of people milling around. It's usually quiet round there but tonight people in jeans were busying themselves rigging up floodlights to illuminate a section of the road they'd covered with fake snow. I found out later that Victoria Wood is filming a TV series in town.

I was riding through the park at 5.30am when I noticed a naked man crouched on a bend in the middle of the path up ahead. It was a cold morning and it was raining steadily. As I approached, two other figures came into view about fifteen yards further down the path. They were wearing bus drivers' uniforms and were stood staring at the naked man. They shouted at me to stay away from him. I skirted around the man and asked him whether he was ok as I passed. He didn't reply.

The bus drivers told me they'd been walking through the park when the naked man had leapt out of the bushes and attacked them. The smaller of the two drivers pointed to the taller one and said, "In the end he managed to smack him in the head — he went down and we called the police. He's been crouched down there ever since."

Someone scratched two stars of David and wrote "God's Children" across the back doors of my van.

This is a letter to god.

I am sixteen years I have no job
my brother has no job to much
trouble in my life ~~for~~ please
help me

At Kershaw Cottrell the receptionist asked me to pass her her hand-bag. It was on the floor on my side of the service hatch. She said the office door had been locked when she'd arrived for work so she'd had to climb in through the hatch but hadn't managed to take her bag through with her.

In the Building Society I heard a woman behind me say, "Bloody hell fire, I want to be in Skipton now — not in this queue."

I knocked on the door of a house on Nelson Street. A woman opened the window of the front room. She was about sixty-five with dyed black hair, red lipstick and chunky gold jewellery. She shouted something to me but I couldn't hear her because of her parrot squawking inside the house. She told it to "shut up" and called me over with the parcel. I told her I'd seen a parrot on my way into work that morning. "What was it like?" she asked. I described it and she said it sounded like an African Grey. "They can't half talk them, you know. You should have caught it — you could've named your price, you stupid bugger."

I explained it had been sat out of reach on top of a street light and besides, where would I have put it?

"You stupid bugger, they're worth about a thousand pounds. You could have put it in your van."

I explained I was on my push bike at the time.

"Well," she said, "you're a stupid bugger and you've got a stupid hat on."

She nodded at my baseball cap. Then she said, "They're all wearing them aren't they? I've got one."

She took the parcel and said, "Thanks. Drive carefully won't you love, you stupid bugger."

The haberdashery on Dunford Bank shut down today. I saw the proprietor while I was emptying the box outside and he said, "It's a licence to print fucking money but I can't be arsed with it any more."

In the smoking room Rod Singleton asked if anyone had seen Christina Aguilera on This Morning.

He said he didn't much care for her face but "Fuck my old boots she's got an amazing body!"

He said he thought she'd have a "massive cunt" and that "if you got down between her legs it would suck you up whole."

He said, "There were some dancers miming sex with her."

He said if he'd tried doing that, his knees would have given out.

He said, "If she had Jordan's tits she'd be the perfect woman — apart from her face."

The headline on the copy of the *Sun* in the Grimscar box was: SINCLAIR ADMITS HE ROMPED WITH RAPE CASE GIRL.

For Sale

P Reg 2.0Ltr
79k Full Service History Taxed and Mot
Excellent Condition
Phone: 07961571738
£1595 ono

I attempted to deliver a parcel to a run-down old shop unit. It appeared to have been empty for some time. There was nowhere to leave the parcel and the front door was boarded-up over the letter box. On one of the boarded windows someone had written "DONT MAKE THIS INTO TAXI".

Someone has written "TWAT" in the dust on the extractor fan above Rod Singleton's chair in the smoking room.

DEBBIE ON BLUE RD

Leave Me Alone And
Dont Play With Me!!

One of the houses on Mason Avenue was on fire.

Ady showed me a video on his phone: a man was having sex with a rubber doll.

When I arrived at work a teenager in a beanie hat was being frisked outside the gates to the yard by one of a pair of mounted policemen.

The policeman performing the search had dismounted, while his colleague held on to both sets of reins. At the same time a middle-aged couple in matching shell suits were vigorously petting the horses. One of the horses sneezed a load of slaver onto the woman's sleeve. She asked the mounted officer whether he had any tissues. He said he hadn't, so she wiped her arm on the horse's neck. The horse bolted slightly, jerking backwards suddenly. The policeman brought the horse under control with a bit of a struggle. "Steady love," he said to the woman.

"Well, I didn't want horse snot on me arm, did I?" she said.

In the smoking room a couple of the night shift processing staff were asking Rod Singleton where he'd been on holiday.

"Kuala Lumpur," he said.

"Have you?!"

"Backpacking," said Rod.

"Wow!"

When they'd gone I asked Rod where he'd really been.

"Blackpool with the Missus," he said. "They're thick cunts on the nightshift, aren't they?"

HOLIDAY CHALETS NR SKEGNESS ...ly Equipped for up to 6.
2 Double Bedrooms. Kitchen/... ...ge with sleeping for 2. Bath or
Shoewer/Toilet. Colour T/V. ...io/Tape deck. Car Parking on site.
Shop, Beach, Pub with Barf... ...estaurant 5 minutes walk away.
Fantasy Island approx 4 mil... ...way. Colour Photo Albums to view.
Terms £80 to £185 per week. ...lt/Late weekends £55/65.
Further Details Phone 0114/... ...465. or 01754/871795.
                    Book NOW at ... Prices.

SLAITH/WTE

Ex: HUDDERSFIELD

ALL DOWN
All Fuck
OFF
(everybody)

While I was emptying the Grimscar box I saw a drunk couple with grey hair and blotchy skin. They were dressed in a bleached-out black jersey and denim, and were trying to help a companion get himself up off the floor of the children's playground where he'd fallen. They made several attempts but were too wobbly. Eventually they gave up, gave him a cigarette and sat on a bench a couple of yards from him while he just lay there smoking.

Inside the box, the headline in the *Sun* was: I WHACKED HUNTLEY IN THE FACE. I DID IT FOR HOLLY, JESSICA AND ALL OF BRITAIN. There was also a copy of *Glamour* magazine in the box today, headline: 1237 HOT LOOKS, CELEBRITIES-A-GO-GO AND GREAT SEX IN 5 MINS, 5 HOURS, 5 DAYS PICK YOUR TIME SCALE AND GO-OH!

While I was writing out a Form-Left on someone's doorstep I noticed somebody had written "I HATE YOU HATE" on their wheelie-bin.

you

smell

of

shit

P.T.O

There was a girl in tears in the phone box outside Dunford Bank office.

An overweight man in his forties wearing a tracksuit and white trainers asked me directions to the sex shop.

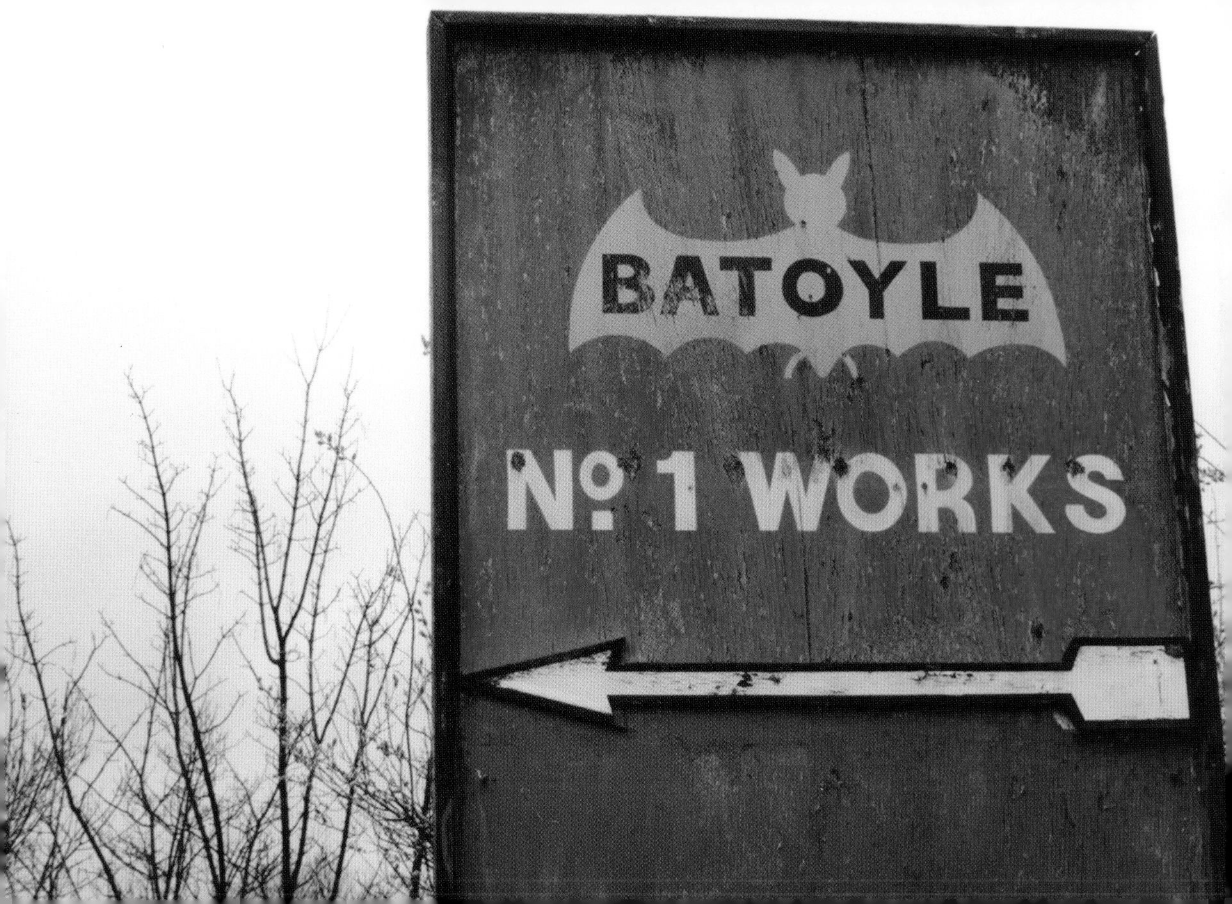
BATOYLE
№ 1 WORKS

I saw a woman walking up Manchester Road with a plastic bag wrapped around her foot. She seemed to know it was there but made no attempt to dislodge it. She must have walked about fifty yards before it blew off of its own accord.

I was riding home when I had to pull up at the lights on Longwood Avenue. While I was waiting I saw the Sikh man who feeds the pigeons on the grass bank next to Kashmir Stores. He struggled across the road with a TV-sized cardboard box before turning it over on the grass, leaving a two-foot bird-seed pyramid. As he wandered back he glanced disapprovingly at the wobbly, rapidly ageing, 1980s New Romantic man who was smashing the receiver of the phone against the side of the phone box from where I often see him making his enquiries. He left the receiver hanging from its cord and aimed a kick at it (which missed) before he staggered off down the street, adjusting his stylish navy blue felt beret as he went.

I've never seen the Sikh Pigeon Man and the Wobbly Rapidly Ageing 1980s New Romantic Man together before.

PINK RIBBON
CASH & CARRY

FOR

WAHL

HAIR·CARE
PRODUCTS

Gentlemen of Leisure

PLAY
WIGS
FROM
£9.99
Opening Times
MON 6.30pm till 9pm
Thus 6.30pm till 9pm

Toilet Roll
PAck of 4
4 Toilet Roll
aH
80P

Someone had forced a potted begonia through the slot of the Grimscar box. The mail was covered in soil and broken bits of begonia.

While I was waiting in the doctor's surgery, an elderly woman came out of one of the consulting rooms, sat down heavily opposite me and said, "I'm dying."

I tried to smile sympathetically. She looked me in the eye and repeated what she'd said.

The woman pulled out a small plastic bag containing a couple of cream crackers from her massive holdall. She untwisted the wire-tie fastener and bit into one of the crackers hungrily. "I've not eaten since half-eight yesterday morning," she said, showering crumbs onto her anorak. "They've told me not to eat owt now, but I'm dying so I can't see as it matters, can you?" she said.

"No," I said.

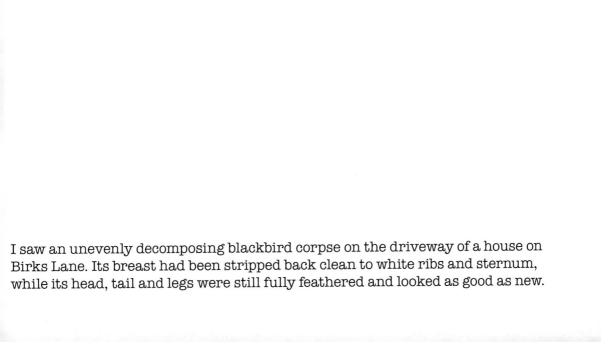

I saw an unevenly decomposing blackbird corpse on the driveway of a house on Birks Lane. Its breast had been stripped back clean to white ribs and sternum, while its head, tail and legs were still fully feathered and looked as good as new.

At a house on Black Moor Road I was unable to deliver a small parcel: it was too big for the letter-box, and nobody answered when I knocked. I noticed an old lady in the garden next door tending the display of square plastic tubs planted up with busy-lizzies. I asked whether she'd mind taking the parcel in for her neighbour. "I don't bother with her," she said, and carried on dead-heading.

Help us improve!

66 Dear customer, I would be happy to hear your opinion about the store. What is good. What could be better. Please write down your thoughts. They will help us improve. 99

Rachel Dodson
Store Manager

Name:
Address:

Telephone: Date:

IKEA Leeds
Holden Ing Way
Birstall, Batley
WF17 9AE

IKEA®
www.IKEA.com

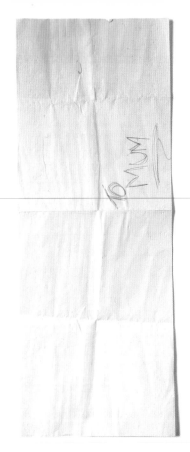

Someone had posted a pair of soiled knickers into the Grimscar box.

I gave Rod Singleton a lift home. As we pulled up outside his house he said, "Rabbit stew for tea tonight."

"Very nice," I said.

"I shot it myself in Tadcaster a month since" he said. "Aye — cut it in half, bang it in the freezer." He paused for a moment then went on, "She suggested having venison. I said, 'No love get that rabbit from Tadcaster out and make a stew.'"

I was stopped in the street by a man with a bogey stuck to the side of his nose and a navy blue jumper.

"Some people have some filthy habits don't they?" he said.

"Do they?" I asked.

"Yeah, people dropping bubble gum on the floor — it gets stuck to your shoes and you can't get it off."

I agreed with the man.

He went on, "I've just seen a lass drop some over there", he waved vaguely across the street. "I says to her, 'Oi! Bubble Gum Face!' and she didn't like it — that's what you should say when you see anyone doing it, call them Bubble Gum Face. She didn't like it at all... See yer," he said as he set off up the road again.

I stopped at the paper shop and bought the *Post*. I noticed a story on page four: "Some people who are over forty went to Hartlepool to take part in arm-wrestling, table tennis, public speaking and reciting from the Koran competitions."

A man in a suit and a navy blue Volvo threw half a samosa out of his window as he passed me on Forest Drive.

23/10/2005

AMANITA MUSCARIA

PAXILLUS INVOLUTUS

DALDINIA CONCENTRICA

RUSSULA NIGRICANS

CALOCERA VISCOSA

PIPTOPORUS BETULINUS

XYLARIA HYPOXYLON

AMANITA FULVA

AMANITA VAGINATA

LEPISTA INVERSA

RUSSULA OCHROLEUCA

CLITOPILUS PRUNULUS

AGARICUS XANTHODERMUS

SCLERODERMA CITRINUM

At the golf club I saw a man walking up the driving range with a radio-controlled golf bag.

A woman with a frizzy perm who smelt strongly of incense asked me whether I'd "seen any snow about." I said there was none on the ground although I had seen a few cars with snow on their roofs. She asked how high up I'd been and I told her "Stile village." She said her son had been in Switzerland and there was some snow there.

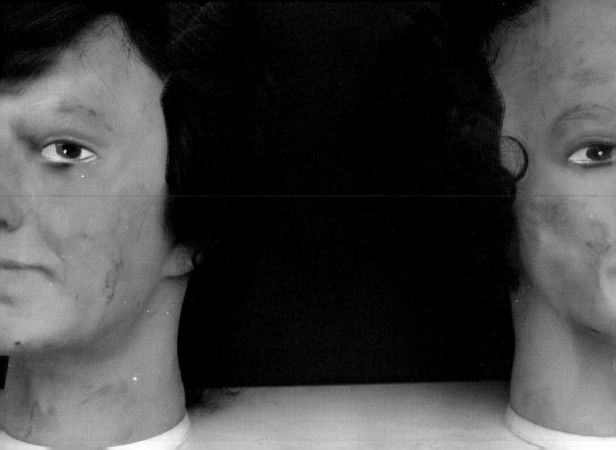

While we were prepping, Charlie Fotheringham was telling me how he'd arrived at a house to deliver a packet and there'd been a note on the front door: "Do not knock at the door — hypnotism in progress."

"What did you do?" I asked.

"I rang the bell," said Charlie.

In the smoking room Ady was sat on an upturned letter tray when Rod Singleton came in.

"You look like a gnome sat there," Rod said.

"At least I don't look like a cocksucker," said Ady.

"At least I'm not a cocksucker," said Rod.

"Fuck off," said Ady.

"Small cock," said Rod.

It was raining steadily as I made my way through the beer garden of the old Bare Knuckle Boys Inn (recently renamed "Bar-celona") with a parcel for the landlord. All the wooden picnic-style tables were empty apart from one; three sixth-formers were sat with a single glass of orange juice between them. They were all smoking and discussing the pros and cons of giving up. One of the girls — with a long, back-combed dyed-black bob and stripy tights — said, "I couldn't give up — no way — I even smoke in the shower." When the slightly camp boy with the thick rimmed glasses and the bandolero-style record bag said, "Really?" she went on to explain, "Yeah, it's the most difficult thing ever — smoking in the shower."

At a house in Fearnley Avenue I skirted around the metal post that had been set into the middle of the concrete garden path to moor the caravan that took up nearly the whole of the front garden. I was in a hurry to make all my "Special" deliveries before the guaranteed 1 o'clock so I was relieved to note someone was in. There was a thin woman with an old fashioned perm and twin-set sat with her back to the window of the front room, and she appeared to be in conversation with a similarly presented woman in the chair opposite. I knocked on the door. Nobody answered. I knocked again, harder. Still nobody came. I could see the back of the woman's head in the window – she hadn't moved. I reached across and tapped on the window. She still didn't move. I stepped closer to the window and peered in: the woman in the window was actually a shop mannequin and the woman across from her was the reflection in the mirror that had been propped against the wall opposite. I quickly wrote out a Form-Left, posted it and left.

Icome work

draw matea madma and write on aside what
is it and draw the thing nextto it
th and th draw the thing m.

While I was emptying the pillar box on Holland Road, I noticed a Royal Mail van pulled up on the other side of the street. I gave a cursory wave as I dislodged some stubborn letters from the cage of the box.

When I stood up I realised I'd been waving to my own van: I'd parked up on the opposite side of the road to usual.

I was attempting to deliver an "Article For The Blind" to a flat in the centre of town but there was no one in. I thought there'd be little point leaving a Form-Left as I knew the occupant lived alone and wouldn't be able to read it. I phoned Chris in the key desk for guidance; he said he had some braille Form-Lefts and to call back at the office to pick one up.

When I got back Chris was on the phone but when he saw me he broke off to instruct Julian to "find one of those braille Form-Lefts we got from Swindon".

Julian began rummaging around in draws and cupboards. After a couple of minutes he surfaced with a standard Form-Left he'd punched a series of crude holes into with the tip of his biro. As he offered it to me through the key desk window his face cracked and he and Chris began laughing. They didn't stop for several minutes.

On my way home from work I saw two men trying to load a large three-seater sofa onto the roof of an old Vauxhall Cavalier with no roof rack. They made three attempts but on each occasion the sofa slid off onto the pavement where, after the third attempt, they left it and went inside a house.

On the way into work I saw a man in town. He was wearing a smart grey herringbone three-button jacket, a pale-blue shirt, buttoned to the top of the stand, a diagonally striped grey and a blue silk tie finished in a tidy half-Windsor knot.

On his bottom half he was wearing a pair of orange jogging bottoms.

An old man came over from the bus stop as I was emptying the Grimscar box. He said, "Ooh let's have a look, I've always wanted to see inside one of them."

The Smoking Room isn't the Smoking Room anymore. I went in there today; the builders are using it to store their hi-visiblity waterproofs, spirit levels, hard-hats and tins of yellow paint.

It still says "TWAT" on the extractor fan though.

Rod Singleton retired today.